FOUNDRY SONGS

Dean Rhetoric is a working-class poet currently living in Manchester. He has previously been nominated for The Pushcart Prize and was a Semi-Finalist for the Crab Creek Review Poetry Prize in 2018. His pamphlet, *Cancer [+Pop Punk]* is available from Broken Sleep Books.

Praise for *Foundry Songs*

Dean Rhetoric's poetry shakes things up. The phrase-making of *Foundry Songs* is visceral and passionate, forging from trauma and poverty 'a pulsing shield of anger'. Routine harm inflicted by modern industrial, political and economic systems is exposed through searing remembrances of the lost. Here too, though, are earthy poems for the 'carelessly alive' that evoke desire with charm and 'picket lines / around the bedpost'. A fierce, important debut.

— John McCullough, *Reckless Paper Birds*

In *Foundry Songs*, Rhetoric channels the blood and guts of the working class into a brilliant collection of uncompromising poetics. A surreal sprint through the graveyard of forgotten towns, the haunted factories, the noise of misspent youth, where adolescence is dragged into adulthood, and identity smashed against the side of a departing train. This is poetry of the soul, of loss, love and reclamation. It is the voice of the unseen grabbing the world by the throat, and demanding that it listens to its story. Make no mistake, this is a blistering debut that does not care what you think, but asks you to feel instead.

— Stuart McPherson, *Obligate Carnivore*

Surprising and exciting poetry, filled with energy, power, and profundity.

— Cathy Bryant, *Best of Manchester Poets*

Dean Rhetoric's *Foundry Songs* are flicks of space caught in the bountiful hands of time. A mind corrupted and refurbished. A soul with the darkness of light. Each poem, a sermon of unravelling - a gorgeous disrobing of invisible intimate parts.

— Ingrid M. Calderon-Collins, *Let The Buzzards Eat Me Whole*

Foundry Songs

Dean Rhetoric

For the Crowsty Boys

Also by Dean Rhetoric

Cancer [+Pop Punk]   (Broken Sleep Books, 2022)

ISBN: 978-1-915079-60-2

The author has asserted their right to be identified as the author of this Work in accordance with the Copyright, Designs and Patents Act 1988

Cover designed by Aaron Kent

Edited and typeset by Aaron Kent

Broken Sleep Books Ltd   Broken Sleep Books Ltd
Rhydwen   Fair View
Talgarreg   St George's Road
Ceredigion   Cornwall
SA44 4HB   PL26 7YH

Contents

It's all wrinkled elbow shirts and poker faces on this bus
Back to a nitch dug just like a ditch in this city's weathered crust
But there's something about this city's grey
That seems to say all there is to say
Riddled with regiment, vindictive intent
Faking loyalty and getting paid
Fuck them all.
       — Dillinger Four, *Super Powers Enable Me to Blend in With Machinery*

I can hire one half of the working class to kill the other half.
       — Jay Gould, railroad tycoon and financial speculator

Love Letter to your Animal Decomposition

Count the times you've attended the death party of a bile duct.
Statistically, you could be invited to one in every twelve hundred gatherings.

On average, it takes twenty months of radiation to change a photograph
into a sympathy card, curling into the fire pit underneath your chin

and swallowed like warm bread of pigmentation. On average,
a friend will offer twenty minutes of emptiness, whispering about the dead

and what a shame it is that we can't make them less dead.
Lungs will be respectfully unbuttoned, hung safely with the catheter.

The fruit platter, sentimental – the apple's eye still seeding.
The solitary pulse of a carnation – a wall, Jackson Pollocked by a fist.

In the garden, a laughing child will be thrown at God by parents.
In the hallway, a mother sobbing in the stretcher marks of a daughter's dress.

This bile duct will stagger to your doorstep, late and upside down for grief,
a drunken black effigy cackling on its arm.

The backscatter of a passing hearse will throw envelopes of light
at the open window, sealed love letters to your animal decomposition.

I won't shout. I won't cry. I will make the opposite of a scene.
It's getting loud outside and your silence has everywhere to be.

EMDR

It happened, alright?
No need to explore the specifics

but crack me a stiff one on the bridge of the nose
and I'll hatch drippings for the windows
to drink their fill of assumptions.

From the safety of the ceiling
come moments
edited with eyelids:

nervous chittering in the walls,
the sting of red brick
on baby tailbone

and pressed stomachs
waltzing violently
with the faint smell of semen.

It was never about rising above the trauma:
It's about what to do with its
pulsing shield of anger

forged in the bowels of the foundry,
and baptised in the wet patch
of the basement mattress.

+ *Psalm of Bandages* +

We needed a distraction and God was
as good as any.

When we hid under chapel stairs,
forehead on forehead.

When your skin was itchy and too tight
for your swelling chest.

You were God's mint filter,
I was Her ashtray.

My humble bloodied knee staining
your Sunday best, as you

slit your index finger over Corinthians
and mixed us as one.

This was not the first time we'd been so
carelessly alive.

We had crushed leaves, tied together at the stem,
sat formless in pews

between the lustrous punch ups of rain
and the melody it made on the windows

just to destroy something wonderful.
There was no salvation come morning,

only the light, naked in our shaking hands,
sick at the thought of reflecting us.

St. Guthlac Street

The boys had been fighting upstairs again,
two-out-of-three falls giddy
in punch-ups
but still sleeping with the light on,
and the lamppost outside, concerned,
all struggle-mouth to articulate
the ways it would be needed
to shine pretty-bastards of light
on their sons,
or the strict wind of a cringing God
to tear great-galloping-shitless
through them
to bite down on their scruffs
guiding them above the frequency of the street
every house, a big, dented radio of warning,
every bathroom, a child in the tub,
inviting every radio he could find.

Euthanise the Creature

Much like the right kind of sex, I smell good
in the unwashed ambience of a Sunday morning
taking a shortcut through the churchyard
and getting home on whatever God doesn't keep.
There are those who will never
catch the scent of it on their tongues
and for that, I am sympathetic as a hallway.
There are nights that I too have stretched my palms
across the neighbouring body to mine
and convinced myself
the innocuous hum of indifference
travelling between us was some kind
of beautiful song in a foreign language.
There are times that I too have fantasised
a call for help at the foot of the stairs
as the hallway and I remain silent.
The both of us, on our backs since birth,
have no business asking anything remain unbroken.

Chest X-Ray

The radiograph fades in
On a starry Night of blood and alloy

Two dirty-bellied clouds of it wheeze
Struggling to expand:
                        Flexing

For the pretty lint that's tap dancing
Down the light of the
                        Hospital blinds

Each stab of breath, with its tutting
                        Of red mist
Each cleave of sinew against the lung
                A deflated flAg

Once-proud sails overlong the horizon
Now winced with compounds:
                        Light shavings

Snowed Feathers beneath the clavicle
                Alongside elements
Cradled in a Tightening windpipe

One morning I'll be discovered:
                        Dull and brief
A Coiled floor of perfect minerals
                        Lifted and free

O

To be as valuable
As the things this body

                Rejects.

All Working Class Birds go to Heaven

Pelicans are a shower of smug bastards:
Designer throat pouches,
indecipherable bird slang

sipping on filtered salt water and lime,
laughing at the crooked seabirds
who graft all day

for the soggy arse end of a chip
only to choke down a colourful toxin
discarded by a dead-eyed nephew.

Birds of a good social architecture
flock together in dark paradigm,
away from the smell of pestilence
that hangs from the clouds.

The beckoning cliffs tease
a scrap of food
or a lump of plastic kitsch
to the gullet.

Another knackered battery
thumps its wings
until broken
where the oxygen goes.

Another working class angel
dumb heavy
with unnatural parasites,
tarnishing up the sunbeams,

slowly stretching
onto the pier.

How to Unlearn Yourself Completely

I am mostly not made of hands,

or whatever thoughts lean on
to numb before masturbation,

or the parts of a body
I have never learned to use,

that shake under the constant weight
of some imagined destination,

of fist prints inside that just won't straighten
no matter how many times

I   punch   punch   punch   them out

I didn't mean to laugh,
slack-jawed at the punctured air,

or the cracked glass between each sleeve
of its gradually bruising light.

Please understand,
if you suffocate these things for long enough,

nothing really hurts.

LadBook

I
Good Lad

I had a friend who loved his country
because it told him he was a good boy

he showed his appreciation
by travelling around the world

doing bad things to other good boys

he considered patriotism a tenancy
leasing each heartbeat until he died

which no good boy thinks will
actually happen

not even if their lives depended on it

II
Comedy Lad

No time for laughter
  in this economy
  mass redundancies
at the punchline factory
  only so many good anecdotes
to go around

when I was 18 years old
I drove forklifts
  in a comedic style
spun kegs of alcohol
  too high into the air

last Wednesday evening
I dropped a tin of peas
  and they finally came
crashing around me

I understand now
how actions of the past
    take time to be heard
how its presence
    can make you question   priorities

I just want what any man does
    a job   a bed that won't smell
    only of myself
somewhere to lay   supine
    a migraine
I can mistake   for applause

III
Beaten Box Lad

Un ts un ts un ts un ts un ts un ts un ts un ts

I walked the steps the other boys stepped
I ate the food the other boys chewed
I bled the blood the other boys bled
I spoke the lines the other boys fed

Un ts un ts un ts un ts un ts un ts un ts un ts

I buttered my head for the headbutters' palate
Embedded my teeth in a knuckle or two
I hoped it would act like a dial of remorse
To alter the volume of violence it threw

Un ts un ts un ts un ts un ts un ts un ts un ts

I yearned for the notion of pride and belonging
Altered perceptions to what they perceived
I took to the role of my needless persona
Like a needle takes to a freshly rolled sleeve

Un ts un ts un ts un ts un ts un ts un ts un ts

IV
Emotional Eating Lad

Everything in moderation
a quarter-bit fingernail

      a small incision at the wrist

just the tip
don't waste the whole blade

      a working man's portion

of dead fish
on sourdough bread

      four mouthfuls are enough

to stay handsome
in the stomach

      burn off what you take in

a little violence is fine
not the entire hand

      two fingers are enough

to slide as light as a crumb
down the throat of the furnace

V
Last Words Lad

I want you to know it was actually me
who found you in the kitchen first,

unconscious, with your eyes rolled back
to the deep sixes in a puddle of piss.

I want you to know I swept up every broken bottle
so the cat could come in for breakfast,

and that I moved her food bowl away
from the trail of blood and vomit on the floor -

I wrapped up the shards of glass
in an old t-shirt and wrote

sharp   be   careful

across its tucked sleeves
before leaving the house that morning.

Trust me - it would feel sarcastic at this point
to clean the litter from your grave.

Closing Time

and my city is a tongue
clucking in anticipation
of chasing the last bus home
on post-orgasmic
Bambi legs
    and yes, come midnight
these knees will hurt
good with the
soft arrogance
of being alive past
eleven on a
Tuesday night
    and it's true there's
a chorus of stitches
where I've sucked gut
too long against the wind
    and it's true that
there are nights
I've touched myself
but stopped before the climax
    as if to teach myself
the beauty of a pause
    as if arthritic stars
might burn away
the softening flesh
around my pelvis
    as if the space
between what was
and what will be
is salting my bottom lip
    and I've been trained
to either bite down
or fast restlessly

on its quietness
　　until yes, my city closes
like a bad mouth
that's done calling out
for someone
to die alone with.

Poem in which I Call Richard Curtis a Cunt

I understand that it's uplifting
for middle class couples
to see the neurotic posh bloke
with the heart of pure gold
win the hand of the
slightly less posh
representation of his
existential dread
as they lock eyes
from across the room
of a stereotype convention

and I understand you enjoy that scene
when they play fight in the kitchen
of his bohemian mansion
and spread studio approved dialogue
over the stale bread of a
heartbeat sandwich
because it reminds you
of the time *you* did something
equally dull and pointless
in the kitchen of *your*
bohemian mansion

but the credits are rolling
the millionaire hippies
have kissed
the crowd
has applauded
cried Morrissey lyrics
until their clothes
are soaked in cliché

and what of us

under the crippling migraine
of minimum wage
studio lights
still waiting
for the perfect coda
to take us all home happy

picture this if you will

two factory workers on strike
kissing beside the kindling
of a burning police car
under a sign that says

'Only a cunt would write a film
where Margaret Thatcher
is referred to as a

saucy minx'

That's not a metaphor

just a fitting end
to a stupid idea

Strike

The government claims that industrial action
has become the shopworn chandelier

from which all working class romantics
hang their galaxies. But I don't care

what the Bullingdon cunts might say:
call sick and cause dissent with me.

New lust, you're a bloody wrong 'un -
the way you set picket lines

around the bedpost, naked and dangerous
as a petrol bomb in Parliament.

I want to rise you up, all cum-dizzy
and magnificent in the morning.

Lock the door and burn the curtains.
Let the neighbours be afraid.

The Butcher's Daughter

lined her stuffed animals against the wall, told me to take my pick.
I said nothing as she tore through its neck, turned my head
at the lick of her flick-knife across its stomach.

I even pinned it down for her, fussed quietly over the chunk of slate
forced into its fur (*my God, we've given it a real-life heart
just to drown it in the Wye*). She pressed into me

as I held it over the bridge - said to be brave. You can't save every
animal from the butcher's hook. There comes a time when
you must learn to discriminate - to establish distance

between the axe, and that which eats the axe. It suffered to the end,
our mouths, rush-clumsy, the clash of unfinished teeth. I admit it.
I liked the taste of your blood on my sharpened breath.

Spit 1 – 0 Foreplay

I want to make you cum on the office carpet
instead of learning to use PowerPoint
be nine fantasies deep in you
and get a free beverage with the tenth
fuck like floodlights
pushing through the cigarette burn
of a hen night cowgirl hat
want your pelvis to do moonsaults
when someone says something
that sounds like my name
to summon demons
in the discount aisle
of a haunted dildo factory
the security camera blushing
like a mad gibbous moon
roleplay as a cloud and hock spitsies
on your freshly scrubbed
back door windows
I need to take you
like a lesson
in writing better similes

Psalm of Bandages II

I

For such a fragile boy
I was doing myself a
mischief with laughter

high fiving the birds
singing along to every
Hail Mary
the *fun* in funeral

said how much fun I'd
had
how he should die again
sometime

heckled the eulogy
to stop being so weedy

after all, there had only
been two deaths
recorded in the history
of the world

Jesus Christ
and everyone else

II

a gap in which I'd lost
friends
so accustomed to
violence
their corpses winced
when the priest
raised a hand
to make the sign
of the cross

can you believe some
people
have such humorous
Gods

as to bury a father of England
decades long
in the dirt

with his fists still
clenched
and not a single worm
intimated

And out Come the Bailiffs

O, how I'd panic right now
if I was enough of a body to be broken

but there goes the last of me
gulped down the plughole
with the bathwater

and these brief, wasted moments of sanity
between God's breath
against the ridge of my wrist

and a rush of sudden debt
knocking violently
against the woodwork

thin as light

And in Come the Toxins

There are over twenty known causes of respiratory disease
in the average industrial furnace   and I'm seven of them
ha ha   seriously though a letter came today   imploring
me to take my breathing issues   in good humour   it can
be fixed   and for only the cheap-cheap price of   well
it's not just about the lack of money   it's the characters
I've created   in this off-Broadway   rendition of organs
if you press your fingers   into your skin   a certain way
and your blood circulation   is bad enough   as you let go
it resembles a kind face   a friend   a troubled life coach
who passes through this oxygen gorging   piggy-piggy
bone marrow   before fading again   into ambivalence
this daddicky chest   clenches   to their aimless ways
like a 2 a.m. jealousy   good sir   your letter   found us
and we thank you   for your concern   about the group
of all the ambulances you've sent   it's by far the funniest

American Thrift Store

in the breast pocket
of a trench coat

a hole
a single spot

furious

lighthouse white

out of which
snuck a quiet boy

who kept to himself
loved his country

fired an encouraging word
between the eyes of
six classmates

before turning the gesture
on himself

On Automatic for the People – By R.E.M

1 – DRIVE.

1998: Kurt Cobain was listening to *Automatic for the People* by R.E.M when he killed himself. I am listening to Kurt Cobain, on my way to find out that you have killed yourself by-

2014: -Hanging up the phone. I offer to move back home and work three jobs so you can focus on chemotherapy. You explain that your new fiancé is amazing and you are-

2 - TRY NOT TO BREATHE.

1998: -the priority is to not cry. Not until I can be alone. I'm scared if I cry, you'll kick the shit out of me again but I look up and everyone is-

2014: -crying. I've slept on their living room floor for almost seven months. Two days without food. You keep asking me to visit you. I'm ashamed to admit that I'm too-

3 – THE SIDEWINDER SLEEPS TONITE.

1998: -broke the headphones so only the left side hears music. I am sent out for listening to it during class. We are learning that suicide is a sin. You are barely even-

2014: -cold outside and six more miles of walking until I get to work. The phone is cut off and you didn't reply to my last three messages. I can't stop my hands from constantly-

4 – EVERYBODY HURTS.

1998: -shaking with rage at the teacher. She leans in and whispers with a smile, *that's exactly the noise your friend would have made before he died,* nobody I tell will-

2014: -believe me, I know the voicemail on my phone is someone telling me that you're dead but I won't listen to it. I can't afford to eat, let alone afford to be-

5 – NEW ORLEANS INSTRUMENTAL NO.1

1998: -depressed, confused teenagers are gathering in a friend's garage. We drink cheap beer and tell cheap stories about you. There is still violence. We are only-

2014: -fourteen miles until home and you're dead and the insides of my thighs are cut to shreds and I can feel blood in my socks and my boots you're dead I can't keep-

6 – SWEETNESS FOLLOWS.

1998: -pretending the music doesn't seem to express everything I want to say about you. A friend offers to put the album onto cassette. It is the sound of a soft-

2014: -funeral happening and I am not there. I am told you are not a relative, no longer my partner and not a good enough excuse to leave work despite our nine years-

7 – MONTY GOT A RAW DEAL.

1998: -later I will wonder if this album saved you for a while, or just made death more comforting. At school, how often did you almost throw the noose around your-

2014: -head submerged under water and the lights are off and the bailiffs are banging on the door and you're dead and I've walked too far and my thighs are-

8 – IGNORELAND.

1998: -badly cut photographs on the bedroom floor. The missed signals. That time you raised your hand in geography and your sleeve slid down. The-

2014: -scars we re-open when the right song comes on. I am fourteen again. I am not crying, nor am I losing weight, there's just less of me-

9 – STAR ME KITTEN.

1998: -existing in this music is something that people feel harmonizes with their death rattle. With which song did you die? Which song stopped you-

2014: -breathing in tune with the banging on the door. The bath is full of blood and I pull keepsakes of cheap cotton out of myself with-

10 – MAN ON THE MOON.

1998: -anything distracting I can get: song of distraction, sing a long scars, song of violence,constant sickening dance of the lost friend still-

2014: -hanging above me on Christmas Eve; your absence howling in surround sound. Your family, scattering piano ashes across the-

11 – NIGHTSWIMMING.

1998: -furrowing of my brow. Your Mother is sobbing. A teenage piano in a coffin. The piano is wearing a scarf so that no one can see its-

2014: -neck bruised, little black octaves blooming under the skin and something about nightswimming deserves a quiet night I won't look away I won't-

12 – FIND THE RIVER.

1998: -look up, I won't ration breath, this perfect environment will not enter me and leave less special. This ghost will not become another carbon dated-

2014: -tremors of your voice, skipping in the groove of the needle. I turn the record over and softly sing back to you, the automatic reflex or memory, both oxygen and jewel.

Donation Box

When I took off your clothes
I hoped the tumor would come with them.

For a while, I even believed it to be true.
The washing machine started to lose weight,

the threads of your favourite jumper
began falling out in clumps.

I cupped my hands across the impression
of your stomach in the mattress

to soundproof it from flipping
when the doctors called.

I practiced how my footsteps
would beat yours to the telephone,

how I'd nail what they cut out of you
to the front door as a warning

to other ailments. Sometimes
I'd hear movement in the kitchen

and find your jeans kick
-thumping with mine in the dryer.

At night, your gloves would
scuttle up the bedpost as I slept.

One covering my mouth. The other,
between my legs; checking.

33

I   *3333333333*   *33333333*
arrive   *33333333333333*   *333333333333*
late   *3333333333*   *33333333*
and

f o r   g e t
t o   b r i n g   a
b o t t l e o f
w h a t e v e r
makes people want to leave a burning house. the hallways are full
of photographs of the ocean in which to drown small, insignificant
parts of   myself and the drawers   are full of
hungry   colourful tablets with   which to
c l o s e hallways of myself in small, insignificant gulps of ocean.
somewhere above us two insects are lost and possibly falling in
l o v e   between a chewed biro   and the ring
of a n   old coffee cup. they are   merely here
to communicate something about the human condition I suspect.
mold waits in bloom and   inside each of the stairs baby
sunflowers reach   out to   the cracks in the kitchen wall
the smoke alarm is well   hidden and screams every
night and it feels forever (33)   in years, minutes or seconds
old toys and insignificant   parts of myself block most
of the fire exits I'll stand   next to the insects and won't
mention the awful smell   hoping they'll be too polite
to notice that I forgot whatever makes people leave a burning house.

Castlefield

Merry Christmas from Manchester
where they believe in the kind of love
that grinds foreheads
and licks the spine clean
but still fucks with its socks on
because it's a British December
and you'll catch your death out   there

I could wax dull about the weather
how it scuffs its heels around the curbs
and asks if you'll visit soon
or tell you I've been wet in my sleep
dreaming of paid utility bills
wrapped delicately in lace
and waiting under the tree
begging me to take them
like a job I don't   hate

Just look at what you've done to me now
wanting you in the laziest ways
familiar and half stale on a Sunday morning
the world slow to fold around the bedroom
cheeks warmed from a heavy breakfast
watching the teenagers on the towpath
run laughing with scissors in love
taking turns to interpret
the Rorschach of their shattered   knees

Pelican Tits

I actually said it   birthed from my mouth   D cups bobbing   against my tonsils
flocking north   to the tune   of my awkward tics   I said it   a disguised sentiment
subtle as a cloud   spraying spit shards   on the fresh paint   of your front porch

I could have said   much more   called you   soft   flickering introversion
perpetual giver   of stomach ghosts   I could have offered   to excite you
under the dinner table   little buildings   of gooseflesh   growing tall

between the hairs   on your forearms   but instead   you got pelicans   oh
and don't forget the tits   a quivering brace   of apostrophes   almost in flight
an inverted climax   cringing   under a dirty great pair   of proverbials

these days   words are dangerous   these days   there are hybrids   in the space
between   each awkward pause   I said it   a baseball bat   of vowels   to the face
pendulous   twin swellings   articulating more   than pelican making words   can say

Love is a Supernatural Bone-Stinker

of an affliction a pesky little earworm
of a condition a shrieking specter
that dares you to lick-pick
at the locks it fastens
on the tip of your tongue
and abide by the promises
it makes on the roof of your mouth
   for the love of God there was a girl
who was beaten for getting pierced
and so she lay in bed all night
picturing her father's throat
whispering   STRIKE   STRIKE   STRIKE
the next day a church steeple
buckled in a storm
and impaled him through the neck
   we could've been time spent
between the bowing of a church spire
and the cleaver it became
you could've touched yourself
and spat mud at the sky
until it   SPLIT   SPLIT   SPLIT
I could've fragmented into molecules
and reassembled on the tip of your finger
   for the love of God there was a hypnotist
who tripped and broke his skull
before he could wake his patient
from her induced sleep
and so she lay there for two days
smiling peacefully beside his corpse
according to friends she was there
to confront her fear of death
   we could've been time spent
between static and decay

a pair of catatonic bone-stinkers
our souls dancing wildly
to the thumping on the front door
the Saturday night television
purring its warm musical illness
you can't tell me you didn't want that for us

Taxidermy & Curiosities

Inside of the shop is a glass cabinet
Inside of the glass cabinet is a fox
Inside of the fox is a glass eye
Inside of that glass eye
    there's a reflection
Inside of the reflection is you
Inside of you is a glass room
Inside of that glass room
    is a replica model of a glass room
Inside of that model is a playhouse
Inside of that playhouse is a puppet
Inside of that puppet is a hand
Inside of that hand there's a bone
Inside of that bone is a fracture
    and in that fracture is a story
Inside of the story is a divorced dad
Inside of that divorced dad is a worry
Inside of that worry is a baby seat
Inside of that baby seat there's
    a divorced dad's worth of sadness
Inside of that sadness is a boy
Inside of that boy is a wolf
Inside of that wolf is a fox
Inside of that fox is a bird
    and in that bird is a house
Inside of that house is a room
Inside of that room is a cabinet
Inside of the cabinet is you
    breath sweating against the glass
    two fingers, drawing in the fog

Again. Again.

We Are Television

6 pm:

We are the coming together of a City after a National Tragedy.

7 pm:

We are a healthy diagnosis after months of uneasy test results.

8 pm:

We collect dead skin on our faces and hoard it like lush confectionery.

9 pm:

We nudge the loudest products into every hollow box until blood shows.

10pm:

We are always there/or bored/then always there/or bored.

11pm:

We require very little effort to maintain.

12am:

We are optional in 987 ways.

1am:

We are ten minutes of almost attraction, nose close to orgasm before we have to pray.

2am:

We are a ten second delay in case of a passionate live outburst.

3am:

We are a sponsored political party campaign, clicking past forming tumors.

4am:

We are rinsed in electric dye and bad for our eyes.

5am:

We are falling asleep to us.

6am:

We are a mass platform that says nothing anymore.

Milk Willow

I fell   and split   my knee   your mother   kissed it better
that night   I imagined her   watching me   through the crack
in my bedroom door   her saliva   drumming   on the floorboards
index finger   pressed softly   against her lips   it's bad

manners   to have had   a childhood   and expect others
to tolerate   its presence   to fill   your pockets
with calcium   and still   leave room   for the erection
beating   impatiently   against your jeans   I came

back   that night   waited   in the tree   my hands
caressing the swell   on the willow   until I fell   and split
my knee   she kissed it better   I should be   ashamed
I thought   the cancer   was going   to kill you

Nostalgia as Acceptable Depression Porn

once a year
the moon parks a big fat shit
in the ocean's mouth
and dares the tide
to try and pronounce your name
as it rolls its tongue
against the shore

you're right

it's pathetic
that I can't simply say

I'm still in love with you
                    I hope you die alone

Amateur Dramatics

Every Thursday, after yoga. Subdue male suicides through art.
Tell that to my neighbour, who in an anecdote that is
sometimes a true story depending on his mood

was held at finger-gunpoint and forced to pretend he was a tree.
Every Friday he'd wake up to find another teenager
swaying by the neck from his extended left arm.

Every Saturday he'd drink to subdue the constant sound of rope
creaking against his bicep. Almost reaching out for help,
but then, of course, not bothering, really.

Me and my Big Fuck-off Nose

are getting dressed up to go out on the town
and indulge in our insatiable appetite
for the knuckle bones of other boys,

to brush the dirt from our cartilage
and accentuate the curves of our septum
until swollen to the point of

agoraphobic sundial, until lost again
in whatever the hell we were before
learning of our intrusion on the world.

Parenthood

1.
I don't need it. I'm already losing sleep
over everything that's ever happened
or existed in the world and can't
make room for more. I resent
the concept of modern babies,
with their punch-drunk swagger
and soft-headed gibberish,
merrily shitting up the curtains
to a standing ovation in the nursery.
Besides, what kind of father
would I have been? I know

2.

What you're thinking: *He'd be parts of you.*
A child deserves better than that, but
I'd teach him about the miracle of dust,
how we shed 600, 000 particles of skin
per hour and how life is about lining up
each piece to protect yourself from
what's coming around the corner.
He'd think his modern baby thoughts:
A million good pieces die to save just one?
It's not enough – then he'd sneeze
and hit my belly like a punchline drum.

Silk Cut

Look, sometimes we let a little trauma
salt the meat of the men we become

when we were boys
every son on the street
was a murderer
suffocating their softest parts
so their friends
had less of them to hurt

unbuttoning buildings
to sneak upstairs
past curfew

if caught
their cries for mercy
were tested on the damn birds
until the damn birds
were broken

Psalm of Bandages III

1.
Everyone's talking about the church
that screamed out at the ceremony

how there's medication to remove
the tongue from the bell tower

and how it's purely a
precautionary measure.

2.
It's October and the trees are cancerous.
Clumps of leaves take sanctuary in the gutters

the boy next door sits guard
on the front porch

catching stray bugs in coffee jars
without air holes

suffocating them
with the best of intentions.

3.
When life comes for him,
with its mad

beautiful vehicles
of unpredictability

I worry over
who'll catch him.

4.

I worry over losing grasp
of the difference

between those who are young
and those who deserve to be hurt.

I worry about becoming
more dead bug

than dead-bug-making saviour.

5.

I swear   I could've heard something

a frantic wing   against the church bell

a brief bother   to its conscience

a word   I couldn't understand

barely   spoken

gone   with the smell of virtue

on its morning breath.

American Remake of Sleep

You're recast as a little white lie
  that snuck in
through a crack in my frontal cortex
    crept along the floorboards
  of the house
I was dreaming up
and threw the daughter
    we'd joked about having
out of the window

in the garden   the foxtails
lined up around the blanket
    anticipating a snoutful
of good blood
    finding only the guts
of a torn bin bag

as you turned to run away
  she appeared
from behind the wardrobe door
    clicked her fingers
and pulled the both of you
    through a mousehole of ether

Crowsty Boys

(Crowsty: Meaning 'bad-tempered' in old Herefordian slang)

There's no word   for saviour   in the working class bible
just a police sketch   a gang   of savage bastards   hoods
held up   tactically threaded   through pinhole-thin eyes
and by   savage bastards   I mean   a bastardisation
by savages   about a cluster   of shivering   boys   painted
violent   through the jittering   of printer ink   there's
no word   for standards   and yet   in the 1998 of myself

there's dad   smoking roll-ups   buttering dry Weetabix
for the nightshift   insisting   it's all the food he needs
to get by   the tip   of his thumb   still earning   its keep
on the shop floor   boys   from these parts   walk harder
across the gantry   boys from these parts   let their steel
toes   pave new roads   boys   from these parts   drag
knuckle   to wet the gears   of production   with blood

A Farewell to Lungs

One unchristian afternoon
I'll accept their resignation

and snip   scissor fingers
through the clouds

for the perfect lungful of sky
to click   into the cleft of my chest

retch my dirty chops up
with the spit's worth of air I have left

apologising in person
to each withered balloon of grief

for having fought so long
against the stuttering blitz of their design

and leave them   shivering against the mesh
of the nearest industrial site

until I fold   in cuts of wet silk

impossible to inscribe
with even the softest epitaph   of murmur

Foundry Song

I

He was too proud for fear.
Never moved from his station.

Instead, the foundry bowed in
respect as the crane snapped,

crushing him against the bricks.
He wouldn't move first,

barely acknowledging the
fingers it took.

II

There is a chain link
branded into my bicep

from where I once
turned my back

on that which
wasn't done with me

and felt it had to put me
in my place.

III
When it's my turn
against that wall,

I won't be so
dismissive

of the parts that
slow me down.

IV
When I am out of ways
to reduce myself,

I'll leave a month's rent
in advance, press the slack

of that chain to my waist and
wait patiently to be scrapped.

V
When I accept my lot,
scatter me obnoxious.

Mould me into something
a child can throw

at the next departing train.
Help the young ones understand -

Nothing passes through here
unaffected.

Acknowledgments

Earlier versions of some of these poems have previously appeared (with gratitude) in Rising Phoenix Review, Five:2:One Magazine, Seafoam, Forest Publications, Resurrection Mag, Crab Creek Review, Listen Softly's Luminous Defiant anthology, Poke, and Pink Plastic House.

This collection wouldn't have been possible without kindness of the following people:

Ingrid Calderon-Collins, Liam Wheatley, Andrew Cavanagh, Sezzie Davies, Scout Tzofiya Bolton, Claire Askew, Malin Nilsen, Stuart McPherson, Sophie Watts, Aaron Kent, Kristin Garth, Wayne-Holloway Smith, John McCullough, Melissa-Lee Houghton, and Kaela Quinn.

Please send all poetry enquiries and death threats to dean.rhetoric@gmail.com

LAY OUT YOUR UNREST

Lightning Source UK Ltd.
Milton Keynes UK
UKHW011019050123
414878UK00004B/164